He who reflects on other men's insight
will come easily
by what they labored hard for.

Socrates

Caldwell van Roden, editor

business: serious activity
requiring time
and effort

acumen: keenness and
depth of perception;
discernment

SEED THOUGHTS

goal: the end toward which effort is directed

One is only properly motivated to achieve a goal when he is able to define it.

Management by objectives gets one to look forward rather than backward.

Duties constrain managers, objectives liberate them.

W. J. Reddin

The more clearly one sees the best method of achieving a goal, the easier it makes doing so.

In the game of business, goal attainment is how the ''score'' is kept.

plan: a method for achieving an end; a detailed formulation of a program of action

An objective without a plan is a dream.
W. J. Reddin

It is far less for lack of intelligence, than for lack of method, that men achieve less than they desire.

All high achievers plan their work and work their plan, for they are keenly aware that ''luck'' is most often being prepared to take advantage of a situation.

Plans facilitate goal attainment.

prioritizing: to arrange in order of importance

First things first.

There is a royal road to anything. One thing at a time, and all things in succession. That which grows slowly endures.

J.C. Holland

He that would do a great deal at once will never get much done.

Effective managers focus on one job at a time, tackling the most crucial one first.

A stitch in time saves nine.

English proverb

analysis: separation of a whole into its component parts; an examination of a complex, its elements and their relations

How little do they see what really is, who frame
their hasty judgment upon that which seems.

Robert Southey

A business man's judgment is no better than his
information.

P.R. Lamont

On the clarity of your ideas depends the scope of
your success in any endeavor.

James Robertson

Failures are divided into two classes—those who
thought and never did, and those who did and
never thought.

John Salak

I had six honest serving men;
they taught me all I knew.
Their names were where and what and when
and why and how and who.

Kipling

think: to determine by reflecting;
to subject to the process of
logical thought

No problem can stand the assault of sustained thinking.

Voltaire

Success doesn't come the way you think it does, it comes from the way you think.

Robert Schuller

A man's [business] life is what his thoughts make of it.

Marcus Aurelius

Where your mind goes, your energy flows.

What you think on grows.

Think.

IBM's motto

"homework": preparatory reading
or research

Chance favors the prepared mind.

Louis Pasteur

It is not the will to win; it is the will to practice to win that makes the crucial difference.

Bobby Knight

I not only use all the brains that I have, but all that I can borrow.

Woodrow Wilson

work: sustained effort to over-
    come obstacles and achieve an
    objective

Success in business is 1% inspiration and 99% perspiration.

Thomas Edison

He who labors diligently needs never despair; for all things are accomplished by diligence and labor.

Menandes of Athens

The three great essentials to achieving anything worthwhile are; first, hard work, second, stick-to-it-iveness, and third, common sense.

Thomas Edison

Don't bother about genius. Don't worry about being clever. Trust to hard work, perseverance and determination.

Sir Frederick Treves

Plow deep while sluggards sleep.

Benjamin Franklin

start: to begin an undertaking

The journey of 1,000 miles starts with a single step.

Chinese proverb

On the plains of hesitation bleach the bones of countless thousands.

Lampis, the ship owner, in being asked how he acquired his great wealth, replied "My great wealth was acquired with no difficulty, but my small wealth, my first gains, with much labor."

Epitetus

Well begun is half done.

Aristotle

achieve: to carry out success-
fully; accomplish

ALL HIGH ACHIEVERS
HAVE FOUR TRAITS IN COMMON

1. They set objectives.

2. They employ the practice of analysis and establish plans distinctly tuned to the situation.

3. They decide how best to allocate their time and focus their energies.

4. They manage themselves by focusing on one task of prime importance at one time.

9

self-management: to provide guidance for oneself

Most powerful is he who has himself in his own power.

Seneca

If passion drives, let reason hold the reins.
Benjamin Franklin

Self-conquest is the greatest of all victories.

Plato

Focus, concentration and constancy, these three, and the greatest of these is constancy.

van R

All high achievers decide, not circumstance, on how best to allocate their time and focus their energies.

effective: ready for service or action; producing a desired effect

An effective manager:

- Does right things . . .
    not just things right.

- Produces creative alternatives . . .
    in addition to solving problems.

- Optimizes resource utilization . . .
    instead of just safeguarding resources.

- Obtains results . . .
    rather than just performing duties.

action: an act of will; initiative enterprise

Nothing can come of nothing.

Nothing will ever be accomplished if all
objectives must first be overcome.

Iron rusts from disuse; water loses its purity
from stagnation; even so does inaction sap the
vigors of the mind.

Leonardo Da Vinci

Heaven ne'er helps the man who will not act.

Sophocles

doing: action; the art of
performing or executing

An acre of performance is worth a whole world of promise.

W.D. Howells

Nothing is so fatiguing as the eternal hanging on of an uncompleted task.

William James

The world is divided into people who do things and people who get the credit; opt to belong to the first class, there's far less competition.

Dwight Morrow

This is a world of action, and not for moping and droning in.

Charles Dickens

effort: use of energy to do something

Oh Lord, thou will grant us everything for the price of an effort.

Leonardo Da Vinci

Life leaps like a geyser for those who drill through the rock of inertia.

Dr. Alexis Carrel

Activity in back of a small idea will produce more than inactivity, and the planning of genius.

James Worsham

Success is due less to ability than to zeal. The winner is he who gives himself to his work body and soul.

Charles Buxton

There is no genius in life like the genius of energy and industry.

Donald Mitchell

The mode by which the inevitable comes to pass is effort.

Oliver Wendell Holmes

participation: to have a part
in something

People support what they help create.

What affects everyone can best be solved by everyone.

You become successful by helping other people become successful.

No general can fight his battles alone. He must depend upon his lieutenants, and his success depends upon his ability to select the right man for the right place.

J. Ogden Armour

Human desires are the stream which makes the enterprise prosper.

time: the hours or days occupied
  by one's work

Time is an equal opportunity resource; no one has enough of it, yet each of us has all that there is.

Time is inelastic; the more inelastic a resource the greater the need to optimize its utilization.

One realises the full importance of time only when there is little of it left.

P.W. Litchfield

Do not squander time, for that is the stuff life is made of.

Benjamin Franklin

By time and toil we sever what strength and rage could never.

Time is the most valuable thing a man can spend.

Theophrastus (278 B.C.)

succeed: to turn out well; to attain a desired end

The secret of success is constancy to purpose.
Benjamin Disraeli

To climb steep hills requires a slow pace at first.
Shakespeare

You become successful by helping other people
become successful.

Nothing succeeds like success.

Dumas

attitude: a mental position
assumed for a special purpose

Nothing can stop the man with the right mental attitude from achieving his goals; nothing on earth can help the man with the wrong mental attitude.

Ziege

Attitude determines altitude.

Human beings, by changing the inner attitude of their minds, can change the outer aspect of their lives.

William James

Aptitude, education and advantage get one started; attitude and effort determine how far he goes.

van R

Where there's a will, there's a way.
English proverb

positive: marked by affirmation;
logically affirmative

The habit of looking on the bright side of every event is worth more than a thousand pounds a year.

Samuel Johnson

Positive anything is better than negative nothing.
Elbert Hubbard

True prosperity is the result of well-placed confidence in ourselves and in our fellowmen.

Burt

You will become as small as your controlling desire; as great as your dominant aspiration.
James Allen

The word impossible is not in my dictionary.
Napoleon

listen: to hear with thoughtful attention

While listening, one learns; while talking, the other fellow does.

Good listeners generally make more "sales" than good talkers.

B. C. Holwick

One man's word is no man's word;
We should quietly hear both sides.

Come now, and let us reason together.

The Bible

There is listening, and there is Listening . . .
The latter is with the third ear.

teachable: apt and willing to learn; capable of being taught

To accept good advice is but to increase one's own ability.

Goeth

He who is not "open to learn," can't.

A prudent question is one-half of wisdom.

Bacon

A man should never be ashamed to own he has been in the wrong, which is but saying in other words that he is wiser today than he was yesterday.

Pape

Minds are like parachutes—they only function when open.

Lord Thomas Dewar

They know enough who know how to learn.
Henry Adams

win win: to obtain by work;
succeed

All of business is finding a need and filling it . . . *well*.

It is never a good deal when only one party thinks it is.

B. C. Forbes

To the degree you give other people what they want, they will give you what you want.

It is in giving that we receive.

St. Augustine

Priority focus:

1. customers
2. employees
3. community
4. shareholders

anger: a feeling of displeasure and hostility resulting from mistreatment or opposition

Acting in anger is like putting to sea in a storm.
Benjamin Franklin

To take action in anger is to put your fist in a hornet's nest.

When anger arises think of the consequences.
Confucius

When angry, count to ten before taking action; when very angry, one hundred.
Thomas Jefferson

The great remedy for anger is delay.

problem: an unsettled question raised for consideration and solution

A problem well-defined is on its way to being solved.

Each of us is either a part of the problem or a part of the solution.

A good thing to remember and a better thing to do, is to work with the construction gang and not the wrecking crew.

The more clearly a problem is defined the easier it is to solve.

The best way out is always through.

Robert Frost

PROBLEM ORIENTED PEOPLE
ADD HEAT

They:

- impede
- exacerbate
- stifle
- complicate
- obstruct
- weaken
- thwart
- obfuscate
- alienate
- frustrate
- ferment
- hurt
- block
- inflame

- defeat

They allow problems to fester, which increases
frustration and constrains output.

SOLUTION ORIENTED PEOPLE
ADD LIGHT

They:

- help
- ideate
- enhance
- improve
- foster
- create
- cultivate

- facilitate
- nurture
- conduce
- harmonize
- alleviate
- promote
- resolve

- solve

They generate answers and produce creative alternatives which solve problems and increase output.

SOLVING PROBLEMS BY
THE U.S. AIR FORCE METHOD

- Identify the problem

- Gather data

- List possible solution ideas

- Weigh options

- Select the best alternative

- Act

PROBLEM and GOAL STATEMENTS

"The more clearly a problem is defined the easier it is to solve."

THE PROBLEM IS:

WHAT WE WANT TO HAPPEN:

INFORMATION THAT I NEED:

overcome: to get the better of; surmount

In every adversity there are the seeds of an
equal or greater opportunity.

Clement Stone

The lowest ebb is the turn of the tide.

Longfellow

A set back is the opportunity to begin again
more intelligently.

Henry Ford

The greatest glory is not in never failing but in
rising up every time we fall.

Confucius

The greater the obstacle the more glory in
overcoming it.

Moliere

tough times: extremely difficult to cope with

Tough times never last. tough people do.
Robert Schuller

It is better to light a small candle than to curse
the darkness.

Confucius

. . . in due season we shall reap, if we do not
lose heart.

The Bible

If there is no wind, row.

patience: not hasty or impetuous;
steadfast despite opposition,
difficulty or adversity

Adopt the pace of nature; her secret is patience.

Emerson

Have patience. All things are difficult before
they become easy.

Saadi

The virtuoso was once an amateur.

Emerson

Patience and time do more than strength or
passion.

Jean de la Fontaine

Genius is eternal patience.

Michaelangelo

He who can have patience can have what he
will.

Benjamin Franklin

faith: belief; trust

Every great enterprise begins with and takes its first formal step in faith.

Schlegel

The errors of faith are better than the best thoughts of unbelief.

Thomas Russell

Our doubts are traitors and make us lose the good we oft might win by fearing to attempt.

Shakespeare

The steps of faith fall on the seeming void and find the rock beneath.

John Greenleaf Whittier

Faith is the force of life.

Tolstoy

focus: sharply or clearly
define; concentrate

One principal reason why men don't reach their potential is that they divide and shift their attention amongst a multiplicity of objects and pursuits.

Emmons

He who considers too much will perform little.
Schiller

He who wishes to fulfill his mission in the world must be a man of one idea, that is, of one great overmastering purpose, overshadowing all his aims, and guiding and controlling his whole life.
Bates

The shoemaker makes a good shoe because he makes nothing else.

Emerson

concentration: direction of
attention to a single object

Concentration is my motto—first honesty then industry, then concentration.

Andrew Carnegie

As the gardener, by severe pruning, forces the sap of the tree into one or two vigorous limbs, so should you stop off your miscellaneous activity and concentrate your force on one or a few points.

Emerson

The first law of success in this day, when so many things are clamoring for attention, is concentration—to bend all the energies to one point, and go directly to that point, looking neither to the right nor to the left.

William Mathews

Concentration is the secret of strength . . . in all management of human affairs.

Emerson

determination: being firm in purpose; a strong resolve

Good luck is another name for tenacity of purpose.

Emerson

Lack of will power has caused more failure than lack of intelligence or ability.

Flower A. Newhouse

Destiny is not a matter of chance, it is a matter of choice.

Still achieving, still pursuing, learn to labor and to wait.

Longfellow

perseverance: to persist in an
undertaking in spite of
opposition or discouragement

The race belongs to the persistent.

Practice is nine-tenths.

Emerson

Perserverance is a great element of success. If you only knock long enough at the gate, you are sure to wake up somebody.

Longfellow

Never dispair, but if you despair, work on in despair.

The force of the waves is in their perserverance.
Gila Guri

pluck: dogged determination

The wayside of business is full of brilliant men who started out with a spurt, and lacked the stamina to finish. Their places were taken by patient and unshowy plodders who never knew when to quit.

J. R. Todd

The door of success swings on the hinges of obstacles.

Many strokes though with a little axe, hews down and fells the hardest timbered oak.

Shakespeare

Some men give up their designs when they have almost reached the goal; others on the contrary, obtain a victory by exerting, at the last moment, more vigorous efforts than before.

Polybius

A pound of pluck is worth a ton of luck.

decisiveness: having the power
of deciding; resolute

Decision and determination are the engineer and fireman of our train to opportunity and success.

Burt Lawlor

By the street of By-and-By, one arrives at the house of Never.

Cervantes

All business proceeds on beliefs or judgments of probabilities; and not on certainties.

Charles W. Eliot

Nothing relieves and ventilates the mind like a resolution.

John Burroughs

method: a procedure or process
for attaining an object(ive)

It is not enough to be busy; so are the ants. The question is, what are we busy about?

Thoreau

Using the most efficacious method is like swimming with the current; you progress faster while expending less effort.

Almost all men are intelligent [enough]; it is method that they lack.

F.W. Nichol

The more clearly we see the best method for achieving a goal, the easier it makes doing so.

common sense: sound and prudent,
but often unsophisticated,
judgment

Common sense is instinct, and enough of it is genius.

H. W. Shaw

One pound of learning requires ten pounds of common sense to apply it.

Horace Greely

Common sense is very uncommon.

Mark Twain

Common sense in an uncommon degree is what the world calls wisdom.

Coleridge

Common sense is the knack of seeing things as they are, and doing things as they ought to be done.

Stowe

understanding: the power of comprehending

To know is not to be wise. Many men know a great deal, and are all the greater fools for it. There is no fool so great a fool as a knowing fool. But to know how to use knowledge is to have wisdom.

Spurgeon

Cleverness is not wisdom.

Euripides

Some people will never learn because they "understand" everything too early.

Hear reason, or she'll make you feel her.
Benjamin Franklin

. . . with all you're getting, get understanding.
The Bible

intellectual honesty: chiefly guided by the intellect rather than emotion or experience; adherence to the facts

Facts that are not frankly faced have a habit of stabbing us in the back.

Sir Harold Bowden

It wasn't until I was in later life that I learned how easy it was to say "I don't know".

Somerset Maugham

Get the facts or the facts will get you. And when you get 'em, get 'em right, or they will get you wrong.

Fuller

amiability: characterized by friendly good will

Public sentiment is everything. With public sentiment, nothing can fail; without it, nothing can succeed.

Abraham Lincoln

Those whom you can make like themselves better will like you very well.

Lord Chesterfield

Small courtesies, small considerations habitually practiced give a greater charm to character than the display of great talent.

Kelty

Be good looking if you can be.
Be clever if you must be.
Be friendly if it kills you.

smile: to appear (and be) pleasant and agreeable

Of all the things you wear, your expression is the most important.

Jane Lane

Few things cost so little and buy so much as a smile.

Wear a smile and have friends; wear a scowl and have wrinkles. What do we live for if not to make the world less difficult for each other.

George Eliot

Smile and the world will smile back.

Only he should be a shopkeeper who has a ready smile.

Chinese proverb

humor: the mental faculty of appreciating the ludicrous

A little nonsense now and then is relished by the wisest men.

Benjamin Franklin

I could not tread these perilous paths in safety, if I did not keep a saving sense of humor.

Lord Nelson

People who laugh live longer than those who don't. Few people realize that health varies according to the amount of laughter.

A merry heart does good like a medicine.

The Bible

Good humor makes all things tolerable.

Henry Ward Beecher

courtesy: marked by respect for and consideration for others

Manners are the happy way of doing things.
Emerson

The simple virtues of willingness and courtesy
will carry a man further than mere smartness.
Davidson

Courtesy is simply doing unto others what you
would like them to do unto you.

Nothing is ever lost by courtesy. It is the cheap-
est of the pleasures, costs nothing, and conveys
much.
It pleases him who gives and he who receives,
and thus, like mercy, is twice blessed.
Eractus Winan

Politeness goes far, yet costs nothing.
Samuel Smiles

poise: gracious tact in coping or handling; a stably balanced state

The important thing is to know how to take all things quietly.

Michael Faraday

One cool judgment is worth a thousand hasty counsels. The thing to do is to supply light and not heat.

Woodrow Wilson

When anger rises, think of the consequences.
Confucius

Second thoughts are ever wiser.

Euripides

Whatever may happen, every kind of fortune is to be overcome by bearing it.

Virgil

courage: mental or moral strength to venture, persevere and withstand danger, fear or difficulty; brave

A decent boldness ever meets with friends.

Howe

Courage in danger is half the battle.

Plautus

Never take counsel of your fears.

Andrew Jackson

I steer my boat with hope leaving fear astern.

Thomas Jefferson

There is always safety in valor.

Emerson

Courage is resistance to fear, mastery of fear—
not absence of fear.

Mark Twain

What a new face courage puts on everything.

Emerson

character: moral excellence and firmness

Every man is the architect of his own character.
George Boardman

Man's character is his fate.

Heroclitus

Character and personal force are the only invest-ments that are worth anything.

Fidelity is seven-tenths of business success.
James Parton

You are today where your thoughts have brought you, you will be tomorrow where your thoughts take you.

James Allen

health: flourishing condition;
well-being

The first wealth is health.

Benjamin Franklin

A few die of hunger; of over eating, a hundred thousand.

Benjamin Franklin

A man too busy to take care of his health is like a mechanic too busy to take care of his tools.

Spanish proverb

He who has health has hope; and he who has hope, has everything.

Arabian proverb

integrity: incorruptibility; soundness

There is no substitute for personal integrity.
Howard Hintz, D.D.

To give real service you must add something
which cannot be bought or measured with
money, and that is integrity.

Donald A. Adams

Always do right. This will gratify some people,
and astonish the rest.

Mark Twain

Never esteem anything as of advantage to you
that shall make you break your word or lose
your self-respect.

Marcus Aurelius

Expedients are for the hour; principles for the
ages.

Henry Ward Beecher

Destiny is not a matter of chance,
it is a matter of choice.